THE BRAVE
NEVER WRITE
POETRY • JONES

Coach House Books, Toronto

second edition

  Canadä

Published with the generous assistance of the Canada Council for
the Arts and the Ontario Arts Council. Coach House Books also
acknowledges the support of the Government of Canada through
the Canada Book Fund.

Some of these poems have appeared (in various versions) in *Acta
Victoriana, The Greenfield Review, Inkstone, Koyo, No More Master-
pieces, Piranha, Poetry Canada Review, Poetry Toronto, Swift Current,
U.C. Review* and *Waves*; as well as the anthologies *Milkweed, Other
Channels: An Anthology of New Canadian Poetry* and *The Toronto
Collection: An Anthology of the New Toronto Poets.* The poems in the
second section of this book were originally published as a limited-
edition chapbook, *Jack and Jill in Toronto*, by Unfinished Monu-
ment Press in 1983, as were the haiku of the third section as *Two Cops
Kissing* by HMS Press in 1984.

LIBRARY AND ARCHIVES CANADA CATALOGUING IN PUBLICATION

Jones, 1959–1994
    The brave never write poetry / Daniel Jones. -- 2nd ed.

Poems.
ISBN 978-1-55245-245-5

    I. Title.

PS8569.0487B73 2011   c811'.54   C2011-901852-7

This one's for Robyn

I wanted to give myself to something,
even something false

– Yukio Mishima, *Forbidden Colours*

Contents

Jack and Jill in Toronto

Two Cops Kissing

Foreword

In the summer of 1982 I decided that I would be A Poet. Since arriving in Toronto in 1977 (ostensibly for the purpose of studying the humanities at the University of Toronto – a worthless undertaking from which I many times withdrew and finally abandoned), I had already written several hundred poems. Yet while many of my friends thought of me as a poet, I had little interest in refining my piles of scribblings, publishing them or reading them in public. For five years I worked at more than twenty odd jobs, spending my many free hours and days reading widely, travelling, wandering the streets and hitting the bars of Toronto, each day drinking excessively – a habit I have indulged in since adolescence. My friends, with youthful aspirations to literature, were mostly off searching for something in Europe; I thought that I might have found whatever it was in the cantinas of southern Mexico and Guatemala. Mostly I wished to do as little as possible in terms of being a productive citizen, and Toronto seemed as fine a city as any for this. If I had any credo, it is best summed up by John Glassco in his *Memoirs of Montparnasse*: 'What do I mean to do with my youth, my life? Why, I'm going to enjoy myself.'

Then, in May 1982, through a government make-work program, I landed a desk job in the office of the League of Canadian Poets. The executive director at that time often said she had hired me because I had a 'cute ass' and I was to do little more than keep out of the way, picking away at such menial tasks as she couldn't be bothered with. I admired her in some respects and the job was ideal. I would wander in late in the morning (already well into the day's drinking), take long lunches at a nearby tavern, and leave whenever I was too drunk or sick to keep up a reasonable pretence of efficient idleness. There was a large library of members' books, boxes of archival material, and a case of good scotch left over from some league function; I spent a pleasant summer absorbing each of these.

And that summer I took a good long stare up the asshole of the monster that had become Canadian Poetry. Prior to then, I had thought of poetry mostly in aesthetic terms. My own poetry was awkward, meditative, written in isolation and often imbued with the spirit of Zen. The poets I naively admired were great men and women, joyous and tragic saints far above the everyday world and yet writing the poems that could change that world. Few of the poets I admired were then members of the League, or at least not active members. Through my participation in that summer's Annual General Meeting, the reading of the office's daily correspondence, and the endless telephone conversations, I discovered a massive and absurd mutual-admiration society where poetry was nothing more than the currency that bought greater currency – grants, teaching

10

positions, writer-in-residencies, government-financed reading tours, sex and ever-elusive fame. Half of the poets had nothing to say and no particular skill in saying it; in a way the quality of the poems was irrelevant. Most were professors, instructors and civil servants; they wanted two things – a career in poetry and as big a slice of the Can. Lit. pie as they could lay their hands on. And these they would get in any way possible. Self-promotion, backstabbing, ass-licking, bitching and fighting for readings and contracts were the order of the day. Canadian poetry had become a huge and corrupt bureaucracy. It was ugly, cynical, full of pettiness and hatred. I loved it. I too wanted a slice of the pie. I was going to be A Poet.

That fall the executive director of the League moved up the ladder of Canadian bureaucratic manipulation and fled to Ottawa. Suddenly faced with having to work if I wanted to stay on, I too fled – back to my old life of relative idleness. I had a pleasant study in the attic of an old house on Bathurst Street south of Queen, a large collection of books, a portable German typewriter, and the beer and wine stores were only two blocks away. From this base of operations, I began to write prolifically, organize readings for myself, occasionally mail stuff out to the literary rags and hobnob with other poets; essentially I was playing the poetry game. In the winter of 1983 Unfinished Monument Press brought out a chap-book of the best of the poems I had written during that period. Most of those poems are reprinted here, in the second section of this book, for the most part unaltered except for errors in the original printing.

From 1981 to 1983 I also wrote a large number of haiku, the best of which were collected and published by HMS Press in the winter of 1984. Most of these are reprinted in the third section of this book, along with the original introduction to that chapbook. It should be noted that dates and the chronology of events mentioned in that introduction are somewhat inaccurate due to my faulty memory and do not correspond with some of what has been written here.

Just prior to the publication of *Jack and Jill in Toronto*, my personal life began to take a rather bad turn. I had destroyed a relationship with a woman I loved, my drinking was completely out of my control, I had no money, was too sick to work and badly in debt. I moved to a rooming house on Adelaide Street and managed to hang on for another several months, borrowing money, playing the horses, often ending up in a detox centre and somehow producing a large body of poems that have never seen print and probably never will. In the spring of 1984 I found myself in the psycho ward of Toronto Western Hospital.

It was during this residency, while in the state of heightened perception only possible during extreme alcohol withdrawal, that I first thought out the idea of a massive book (originally something on the scale of Progress Publishers' collected writings of Marx) to be called *The Brave Never Write Poetry*. In May, when I received the first of several honourable discharges, I typed out some of the poems I had been composing in my mind. Then I didn't write for a long time. Early this spring I wrote the last of the twenty-five poems contained in the first section of this book. Now I've rewritten everything a few times and collated it and this is all there is of that great idea that I can barely remember now.

Some of my friends find these poems depressing and 'confessional.' I find them all rather amusing and the protagonist is a stranger to me, though (coincidentally) I seem to have done most of the things he's done and know most of the people he knows. All of the poems that are obviously bad have been accepted by various magazines and anthologies.

With the publication of this first major collection of my work, completed with the assistance of a government arts grant, I suppose I have joined the ranks of the 'career' poets. I doubt that this will inspire great joy among my new colleagues; I'm not sure that I'm too happy about this myself. Every day I tell myself that I will never write another poem, yet again and again I find myself at the typewriter. Perhaps I just have nothing better to do. Perhaps I somehow believe that if anything can save this mad world, poetry will. I'm not sure I care about saving the world. I don't know anything. I'm twenty-six years old now; sometimes I feel fifty-six. I've been off the booze for several months. If the liver and brain can hold out a bit longer, you can expect more of the same soon.

Jones
College Street, Toronto, 1985

THE BRAVE NEVER
WRITE POETRY

The Brave Never Write Poetry

The brave ride streetcars to jobs
early in the morning, have traffic accidents,
rob banks. The brave have children, relationships,
mortgages. The brave never write these things
down in notebooks. The brave die & they are
dead

It takes guts to watch television,
get your hair done, have a barbecue. It takes guts
to blow up the Canadian bomb factory & plead guilty
to twenty-five years

Josef Brodsky was exiled for his poetry & now he
lives in the land of the brave. They like his
poetry there. But the brave don't read it &
in Moscow they are lined up in the streets
to buy food. It takes guts to know some happiness
& not make a poem of it

                      & alone in my room
I am calling someone now, anyone. Someone give me
the strength to be & not question being. Someone
give me the strength to stay out of the cafés &
libraries. Someone give me the strength not to
apply to the Canada Council for the Arts. Someone
give me the strength not to write poetry

But nothing. No one. The streets have not
exploded. The streetcars pass. The clock has
moved another inch

Ernesto Cardenal will no longer write poetry while
the U.S. makes war on his country. I read this
in *Playboy* magazine. Later I stare at the image
of a naked woman, her legs spread across the
centrefold & I know, as the semen runs into my hand,
that she would never write poetry

It is springtime in Toronto. I am in love.

Two Poets

A couple of afternoons a month, we
run into each other at the post
office. Silently we sort through
the contents of our boxes, looking
for the returned manuscripts, looking
for the cheques
     & then the rejections:
 'Sons of bitches don't know good
poems from their arseholes'
        &:
 'So & so's too busy diddling
his secretary to know when he gets
the real thing'
     Or:
 'Goddamn academics, they should
all be lined up & shot'
       Sometimes a
small magazine takes a poem or
there's a cheque & we walk up
the street to a bar & over beer
the talk turns to the women who left,
the races that were fixed, past-due
bills & whatever the bloody Americans
are up to now
      His hair is going &
his stomach & his hands shake now
when he lifts his beer
       & we drink
the beer & talk until the bartender
cuts us off & we stumble uncertainly

onto the street & home to our separate
apartments, where we will sit all night,
drinking coffee & smoking cigarettes,
writing the poems that will make us
immortal.

Better Living Through Chemistry

Toronto was starting to get to me,
I was feeling hemmed in, bored,
maybe even murderous. I went to see
a shrink
       'What seems to be the
problem,' he asked
            'Well,' I said,
'it's like this: everyone I meet seems
to write poetry. They're everywhere,
they're suffocating me, you can't know
how awful it is'
        The shrink leaned back
in his chair & closed his eyes. After
a while he stirred & began to mumble:
                'Um ...
schizophrenic paranoia ... stelazine'
               He wrote
out a script, shook my hand & went back
to his notebook. I looked down
as I was leaving: he was writing a poem.
I rushed to the pharmacy

          I went to a
coffee house a few weeks later. There
were thirty people sitting around, drinking
herbal tea, looking bored, hunched over
notebooks & briefcases. One by one they
went up to the mike & read from pieces of
paper:

one man's woman had left him & he
couldn't find another;

        another had experienced
some sort of existential enlightenment while
sniffing a pine cone;

       one woman remembered,
with tears in her throat, the death of her
grandmother

     It was all very beautiful. I
felt wonderful. I sang quiet praise to the
stelazine. There wasn't a poet in the bunch.

A Brief Affair

I got out of bed & went into the toilet
to piss. When I got back, she was at
her desk, writing in a diary. After a
while, she went into the toilet. I opened
her diary:

> *31 December 1984:*
> *Sex with Jones. He was reasonably*
> *attentive. Quite pleasant.*

We smoked a cigarette & went to sleep,
back to back. In the morning, I went
home & wrote this poem.

Our Generation

In the end it was the fear
of annihilation that did us in.
The vast majority never got over
the second war & slowly melted
into their television sets. For the rest
the process was slower. It was
the loss of hope that got us first &
then the fighting among ourselves. We
turned from our separate tracts & alone
our livers died. We no longer slept or
slept too much. Soon our nerve went &
our limbs shook perceptibly. Our eyeballs,
wild & loose in their sockets, popped
right out. Our minds fused together into
one repeated nothing. We collapsed from
the inside. We'd forgotten how to love
so there were no children. Only the roaches
were left & a few scattered poems, testaments
to our blindness.

Benzedrine

In the evenings we sit in cafés
talking artists & revolutions, of
what we could do, of what we will
never do, drinking beer to mask
the emptiness of our words
                                    Sometimes
it is only the benzedrine that keeps
us going
              & at night with lovers
we no longer want
                          but need
                                      Or at windows
with poems we no longer believe in
                                          It
is the silence that we fear
                                  & the slow
strangulation of daytime jobs that
are not what we were taught
                                      This is all
that we want but this is not what
we want
              Perhaps only a little peace
from a terror that we cannot
comprehend
                    There is no terror
                                        There is
nothing

24

Give it back to us now, give
it whatever it is, as beautiful, as
brutal, as meaningless
                    Give it back
whoever you are
                    billboard signs, shopping
malls, fire engines & the night.

Work

I picked up a temporary job with the League
of Canadian Poets & the night before I
was to start I borrowed twenty bucks
against my paycheque & went out to drink

   The next morning I was sick &
an hour late. My desk was covered with
books that had to be bundled & mailed
out. I smoked a couple of cigarettes
& read some of the books. People were
running around talking about arts grant
deadlines & various problems with the
photocopier. I lit another cigarette &
started to bundle the books. After I'd
made about three bundles I walked down
to the post office. On the way I went
into a tavern for a beer. It went down
quickly & I had two more
                                    When I got back
to the office, the phone was ringing. I
picked it up: some poet from the U of M
couldn't make a reading:
                                    'No problem,' I
said, 'no one would have shown up anyway'
   The phone rang again: she'd written
a book of poetry & wanted to know what she
should do with it. I gave her the address
of the poet from the U of M & suggested she
mail it to him

The other people in the office
were looking at me strangely
                          'I'm going for lunch,'
I said & walked out

                    I went back to the tavern
& had two more beers. I should eat something,
I was thinking, but it was too late: I
walked out of the tavern & puked on the
fresh snow & some pigeons walked towards it
                                        It
was a good sunny day. It was good to be working
again.

A Funny Thing Happened When I Pointed a Gun at My Head

Another love affair had ended & I was out
of cigarettes
                    I walked down to Queen Street
& bought a shotgun & a hacksaw. I drank
a beer & sawed off the end of the shotgun.
I drank another beer & put the shells in.
Then I put a record on and & sat down to relax.
I put the gun in my mouth but decided to have
another beer. I put the gun back into my
mouth but then got to thinking, 'Maybe I
won't shoot myself but just write another poem
instead'
                    But it was too late, someone must
have seen me through the window or something
because just then two cops walked into the room
pointed their guns at me & said:
                                        'Okay, drop it'
    Two fat cops, with bits of steak
sandwich stuck in their teeth, two fat cops,
whose wives had never had an orgasm & if I
shot myself they would shoot me again
                                        '*This*
is poetry material,' I thought as I shot
the two cops. They were dead. I sat down at
the typewriter to write this poem. The grey
kitten came in & climbed onto one of the dead
cops: it began to play with the flap of the
cop's jacket. I worked the poem through:
once again, life was holy & I was immortal.

Like Old Times

In a tavern where we sat
years ago, we drink beer
once again & talk about
those years which somehow
seem so much better now:
Scott, smug but tired,
a professor, a husband;
Martin still looking for
something he cannot comprehend;
myself, scarred with loneliness,
poetry, alcohol

Somehow a woman joins
our table & we are glad. She
is tall & thin & wears a black
dress

'I simply love scotch,'
Isadora coos. 'I love the
people one meets in bars,'
she says. 'You are very nice
boys,' she says

'You're beautiful,' Martin says.
She is. It isn't for a while that
I realize she is really a man

When the bar closes, we charge
drunkenly into the street,

a bit of the old excitement
back & Martin smashes a beer
bottle against the sidewalk.
'I love Isadora,' he yells.

& it is Scott who breaks
the news. 'She is a he,' he
says

Martin looks down at the broken
bottle. 'I never should have left
the airforce,' he says.

Jelly Beans

Jane was a waitress in a vegetarian
restaurant; she was tall, anorexic,
slightly neurotic. She could talk
for hours & say nothing. I thought
it was the real thing this time

It was her brother's birthday & we
went to her parents' home somewhere
in the suburbs. There were little
tables everywhere covered with objects
from China, Africa, India; there were
rare prints on the walls. We sat
drinking Cointreau & out came Curtis's
birthday cake. He was only eleven
but there were at least two dozen
candles & it was spotted with
jelly beans
   'I love jelly beans,'
Curtis said. He blew out the candles
& everyone clapped
     'Light them again,
I love to blow the candles out,'
Curtis said. The candles were relit
& he blew them out again
      'We can't
eat it,' Curtis said, 'it's too
pretty'
  'Of course we won't eat it,'
Curtis's mother said. 'Curtis is going
to be an artist,' she said to me,

                             'I
want to be the prime minister,' Curtis
said

    'Of course you'll be the prime
minister,' Curtis's mother said

Jane was silent throughout the long
subway ride to her apartment. Later
the lovemaking was furious & we lay
in bed afterwards, a bit surprised
about it, smoking cigarettes

                        & then she
started to cry & beat her fists
on the bed:

               'I hate Curtis, he's a brat,
I hate him & I hate my family & I hate
birthdays & I hate being a waitress &
I hate your drinking & I hate your
doing nothing, I hate you, I hate you.'

    'Don't touch me,' she said, 'don't
ever touch me again'

                    She cried until she
fell asleep. She looked very peaceful
lying there in her yellow t-shirt,
her hair cropped short, her blue
bikinis. I lay awake for a while. The
loneliness was slowly coming back, like
an old friend. It was the beginning
of summer.

Steaks

So I met this woman at a party, she
worked in a health-food store somewhere
& was into the tarot. I managed to get
her number before she disappeared

    Brad called early the next morning;
he'd been at the party & wanted the woman's
number. I gave it to him & went back
to sleep

        Brad called again:
                  'She's coming
to my place tonight for a barbecue,' he
said, 'the thing is she's coming 'cause
I told her you'd be there'

                  'All right,' I
said, 'I'll be there'

              'Okay, but look, Jones,'
he said, 'it's my house & I'm interested
in this woman, so don't interfere'

                    'Is there
going to be beer?' I asked

                'There's lots
of beer,' he said

        'I'll be there,' I said

She was sitting on the patio, listening
politely to Brad when I got there. Brad
was explaining Hegel & talking about his
work with the unions. She looked bored.
I was bored. Only Brad wasn't bored.

                                    We ate
steaks & drank the beer. It was a beautiful
evening. We listened to some reggae tapes
& got a little high. Brad was speaking softly
& intently & the health-food woman seemed
mildly interested. It seemed they were
going to do it, for whatever reason. I
supposed you didn't need a reason

                                    I
finished the last beer & got up to leave.
Brad shook my hand:
                        'Thanks for coming, man,'
he said. 'I really appreciate it'
                            I walked
down the street. It really was a beautiful
spring evening. There were times when you
could actually like this city
                            I was on my way
home to my apartment where I would sit &
write the poems of my desperation, of loneliness,
of my ever-impending suicide. It felt good
& right somehow.

On the Beach in Puerto Angel

On the eighteenth day I got it
bad, lying all night on the beach
in Puerto Angel, holding my stomach
in like a shark gone mad, sweating
in the cool air;
                        four thousand miles
by train, by bus, by cattle truck
only to swear at the stupid stars,
the sickly insistence of the waves
in which I crouch for hours, my
bowels emptying into the ocean
                              &
a rooster crowing too, in the yard
of the abandoned naval station
& his screams answered all through
the outer hills of the Oaxacan valley:

this is a loneliness like no other
& a fear & this night I will
remember always
                        & the morning sun
too, burning the leaves of the
crippled palms, lighting the remains
of gutted turtles lying scattered
across the beach of Puerto Angel,
the port of angels.

A Cold Ear of Corn

Blackbirds filled the trees like insane
fruits, the evening air dense
& still; young men & women formed lines across
the *playa* & slowly promenaded, the elders
watching, silently;
in the distance the dark peak of Popocatepetl
    Twenty years old & lost
in Cuernavaca, tired from a day's search
for a ghost I didn't find, a long
month alone in a strange country, I sat drinking
tequila from the bottle & Enriqué
sat down beside me
                    Our conversation
was awkward, there were so few words
we shared, but later we walked through
the market & Enriqué bought a postcard
of the volcano to give to me & I bought a cold
ear of corn & he ate half & then laughed
as I winced at the bitter taste
of lime & chili
          & later still
in the Hotel American I stood
looking from the door of my room at the chickens &
parrots in the courtyard & Enrique came
up from behind & grasped my shoulders
                  & for the first
time I kissed another man, tasted his heavy
tongue in my mouth, felt
the down of his adolescent beard against
my lips

Enriqué's dark hands held my chest
to the mattress as he rode my wanting cock & I cried
out & was gone inside of him. But then I
would not let him enter:
                    'Mas grande,'
I protested & holding his cock in my hand
I began to stroke until the semen shot onto
my stomach & he fell beside me & we
slept
        & in the morning, silently I dressed
& rode the first bus out of Cuernavaca. I
was sick & confused & when I came to the
border of Guatemala I took a new hotel &
for three days drank. One night I fucked
a prostitute & many more days passed
in idleness, drunk

                    Enriqué, six years
have passed as I write these words. I have slept
with many women, lived with some, loved
a few. But on many tired nights alone
at my desk, in dozens
of small rooms in the city of Toronto, the
poetasters & their students staring
over my shoulder, I have sat with memories
of that night & the poems have often been
for you
            I ask only that they might stab
the dumb & sterile darkness hard
as your cock, sometimes splattering small pearls
here & there.

Fried Chicken

Five girls in private school uniforms
in the back of the Carleton car, eating
fried chicken from a cardboard box:
                                    with
manicured fingers they lift the legs
to their lipsticked mouths & tear the
juicy meat away. The smell of chicken
permeates the streetcar
                        I hunch down
in my seat, riding the car to nowhere
in particular, to do nothing in particular,
mentally dividing my welfare cheque into
boxes of chicken
                    Madness will do this to you
& doing nothing & no money & no women, all
of this will do it to you
                                & the girls giggle
& make jokes about the boys in school. They
leave great pieces of flesh still on the
bones & toss them back into the box, among
greasy french fries & uneaten coleslaw
                                        At a
stop I do not recognize, I leave the
streetcar to wait for another going in
whatever direction.

Morning Poem

The sun rests in the top of
a distant factory chimney.
A robin stands in the wet
grass of a park
                 Carefully
I lift the bird upon my finger
& give it to an old man who
is collecting empty bottles.
Without speaking he takes
the robin firmly in his right
hand & places it inside a
plastic grocery bag.

Rock & Roll

When I came to, I was sitting on a
concrete shelf. It was the 52 drunk tank
again & I didn't even try to remember
why. After a while a cop unlocked
the door:
      'Get your stuff & get out of here,'
he said
      I signed for my belt & wallet. I
had a dollar left & I threw it on the
counter:
      'Thanks for the service,' I
said, 'though you should check your clientele,
the man next to me was obviously drunk'
                        I
walked straight out onto Dundas. It was
a sunny morning. I puked into a small
blue garbage can

   I had a reading to give that night &
spent the day pacing my room. It was no
good, I wouldn't make it. I tried to eat
but it came right up. I found a twenty &
went up the street for a bottle. When it
was dark I grabbed the poems & got the
streetcar
      It was standing-room-only
when I got there
         'You're on in ten minutes,'
they told me, 'right after the first band'

I found the bar & ordered several
bottles of beer. There were a couple hundred
people. They were dressed in leather, some
had dyed mohican haircuts. The band was
playing & they were dancing. I swallowed
a couple of valium & drank a beer

                              Then
it was quiet & I heard my name over the PA
& several men in leather were leading me
onstage
                There were microphones everywhere,
the lights were hot. I drained another beer
& stood looking out at the darkness. Then I
fell over. I fell onto one of the drum kits;
a microphone fell on top of me. The darkness
was silent
                I stood up & walked over to
a mike:
                'Now for the poems,' I said
                                        I could
hear myself through the monitors. I started
to read the poems. Silence
                                'Rock & roll,'
someone yelled
                'Up yours,' I yelled back &
then I read the poems through & they shut
up for a while
                & it was over & I made
my way through the crowd. The local radio
station wanted an interview; strangers

handed me beer. I found the back corner
& took a long gulp
                        A young woman in
tight jeans walked up to me
                                'I want to
hug you,' she said
                        She hugged me
                                'Please
don't keep drinking,' she said, 'please
don't kill yourself'
                        It was funny. I'd
forgotten all about suicide. It wasn't for
another two days that I slashed my wrists.

Sweating It Out

I sit in the detox all night,
sweating it out, on the edge
of the DTs & in the morning
they send me by cab to the
emergency ward
                        I lie on a stretcher
& watch the mangled bodies
going past; every few minutes
a nurse takes my pulse
                        'How'd ya
get yourself like this so young?'
she wants to know
                        'It wasn't
easy'
        'What do ya do?' she wants
to know, sticking me with the
vitamin shot
                'Nothing'
                                'No
wonder,' she says. She gives me
some librium. After a while
they put me in a cab & send me
back to the detox

There's a new crowd in, watching
the television, drinking coffee.
I find the tobacco tin & roll
a cigarette. One of the attendants
comes in, Gloria: she is carrying
a cake; there are candles on it.

Gloria brings it towards me
                            'We
found out from your records,' she
says
        Gloria cuts the cake. It is
vanilla with a sickly lemon icing.
It is just like every cake of my
childhood; it is just like any
cake anywhere in North America. We
eat it with shaking fingers. No one
says anything. A couple of drunks
grunt in my direction
                        I get up
& go to the can & puke the cake
into the toilet:
                        I'm twenty-five years
old. I have a long time to go.

Detoxication

Nicky & I are
sitting on a musky sofa
in the dark: it is a
hallway or something
                   We are
smoking cigarettes, it is
sometime in the morning
                   At
intervals the doorbell
rings & the attendants admit
another drunk, sometimes barely
conscious, sometimes in pairs
singing
         They lie down on
the sofas, the snoring comes
on like traffic
              'I've been off
the stuff for three days,'
Nicky says, 'I need a fix
bad'
        An old man stands &
falls down & Nicky stands
& helps him back to a sofa:
when he sits again, the
shaking is worse
              'If I don't
find a place to go,' Nicky says,
'they're sending me back to
fourth floor'

'It will kill
me,' Nicky says. 'Give me
another cigarette.'
                    'It's all
that keeps me sane,' Nicky says

    And outside the streetcars
violently take the tracks as I
concentrate on the burning end
of Nicky's cigarette.

Breakfast in Rockland

'All right, who stole the menu
sheets?'
            The fat nurse in the doorway
glares through the patients. Eight
in the morning & I choke on my cigarette.
Rick laughs, spitting out some coffee.
The nurse directs her boredom at
the two of us now:
                        'They were on
the meal cart & now they're not,'
she says
            Rick stands & raises his
hands in surrender. I light
another cigarette & try not to laugh
but she is hysterical now & begins
to search the room. Someone has left
a tray on a table & she looks under
that & then through the magazines &
the records & then under the tray
again
        'You'll get no meals until
they're found,' she says
                            & soon
there are nurses & assistant nurses
& student nurses throughout the
room, searching the magazines, the
records, each one stopping to lift
the suspect tray
                    Finally the head
nurse enters. He stands in the

doorway, saying nothing, staring:
he'd like to see us all handcuffed,
permanently. I point to the
abandoned tray:
                    'Perhaps they're
under there,' I suggest
                    He looks
dubious but lifts the tray & then
furious strides out of the room:
    'Jones, I know you hid those
goddamned menus,' he says

    Later I see him pacing the
floor of the nursing station & he
glares at me as I pass:
                    'Jones, with
an attitude like yours, you'll never
get out of here,' he says
                    I light
a cigarette & look down at my stitched
wrists: I know that I'll be leaving
& I know that there will be no
more suicides
                    But old Gaetano knows
nothing & they find him later, lying
in his bed & screaming, 'Baba ...
baba,' the meal sheets clenched in
his trembling fists. He had wanted
something to read.

Louie

He drove hack for thirty
years & lived alone
in a room. He never
married
        Now Louie sits
in a plastic chair in the
psychiatric ward, smoking
cigarettes he has bought
with his fifty-three-dollar
government cheque
                'I'll tell
you a secret,' Louie says,
'God is coming back to earth
next week'
        'Don't tell anyone,'
Louie says
        'I've got no blood,'
Louie says, 'there's nothing
wrong with my mind'
             He lights
another cigarette & crosses
his legs, the price tag
still stuck to the sole of
his shoe.

Justina

In the garage of her
house in Scarborough, she
took an axe & sliced open
her own head, but Justina
does not remember this
                          She
remembers the farm in the
Ukraine, she remembers the
sheep, the potatoes, the
cold winters
                  She stares
through the window at
the shovels digging into
the earth: this is where
the new hospital will be
                            The
husband sits staring at
the broadloom, he is holding
a box of chocolates
                          Justina
adjusts the bandage on her
head, as if it were an old
cotton scarf.

Oranges

She is seventeen & she brings
oranges & flowers & wears a dress
the colour of the flowers & suddenly
I feel like a poet again, laureate of
the psycho ward, talking writers &
painters
    till the nurse comes in with
her little blue book. She looks at
my friend & retreats a few steps, then
whispers:
    'Have you had a BM today?'
           My
friend is confused & I pretend to be
as well & now the nurse turns red:
         'Have
you had a bowel movement today?' she
asks & avoids my friend's face
        'Yes,'
I whisper, 'I shat'
     & the nurse makes
a check in her book & hurries over to
Louie:
   'Louie, have you had a BM today?'
she asks
   Louie smiles & starts to count
on his fingers:
     'Yeah,' he says, 'I had
one at nine & another at three, I guess I
had five altogether today'

　　　　　　　　　　'That's more
than yesterday, isn't it?' he asks
　　　　　　　　　　　　　　　The
nurse checks her book:
　　　　　　　　　　　　　'You said you
had four yesterday,' she says
　　　　　　　　　　　　　　　　'I thought
so,' Louie says
　　　　　　　　　　　'That's one more
than yesterday & I might still have
another,' he says
　　　　　　　　　　　　& the nurse moves on
& I guess poor Louie is truly crazy &
I wonder what goes on in his mind
　　　　　　　　　　　　　　　　& I
continue to talk writers with the seventeen-
year-old & she tells me about the
university & about the books that she
is reading & she tells me that she
wants to be a poet
　　　　　　　　　　　　& I peel an orange
& take a bite. Outside the window steam
shovels claw the soggy earth, digging
a hole for another psycho ward.

After Forty-six Days on the Psycho Ward

I have learned to keep silent.
I have learned to trust no one, to
hide my money beneath the potted
plants. I have learned to write
my poems in code. I have learned to
count my cigarettes & empty
the ashtray. I have learned the
importance of three meals a day. I
have learned that Jesus loves me,
for the television tells me so. I
have learned the meaning of doors
& windows. I have learned to
brush my teeth. I have learned to
ask permission to shave. I have
learned the dangers of electrical
appliances. I have learned that
my room must be vacuumed at 6 a.m.
because of experiments by the CIA;
that the beautiful therapist, Nadia,
is in fact a Russian spy. I have
learned to pretend to sleep under
the flashlights of the nurses. I
have learned never to sleep. I have
learned to mark the time of the day,
the days of the week. I have learned
to bark at prescribed times for pills
in a paper cup. I have learned not
to hate, or at least not to express
hatred

After forty-six days on the psycho
ward, I have learned not to laugh
when no one else is laughing.

White Bread

Everything was black, no, it was nothing
at all & then it was too bright & I recognized
the face that was speaking down at me:

'Do
you know where you are?'

'Yeah,' I answered.
There was an IV tube stuck in my arm &
a strap across my waist. The doctor shone
a small light in my eyes

'You took a deliberate
overdose,' she said

I watched her lips; the
lipstick was perfectly applied

'The ambulance
driver found this poem beside you,' she
said

I didn't say anything

'How long have you
been drinking this time?' she asked

I stared
down the line of her neck to where the skin
disappeared beneath her coat

'You've been
having convulsions,' she said, 'you should
eat something'

'I couldn't eat'

'Then we'll
have to stay with the IV,' she said

'Okay,
I'll eat'

        She pulled the IV out of my arm
& moved a table beside the bed. There was
a styrofoam cup, it smelled like instant
coffee & a sandwich wrapped in cellophane,
something in white bread & two slices
of carrot
            'I can't eat this shit,' I
said
        'That's pretty funny coming from someone
who just tried to kill himself,' the
doctor said
                I started to unwrap the sandwich;
my hands were shaking badly
                            'This is your
third time in this hospital,' she said
                            I looked
down at her waist; she was wearing a black
leather skirt
                'I'll have to move to a different
neighbourhood,' I said
                            'You think suicide
is funny?' she asked
                        I took a bite of the
sandwich; it tasted like plastic
                            'Do you
still want to kill yourself?' she asked
                                'No,'
I said, 'three strikes & you're out'
                                I
swallowed some of the coffee; it was sickeningly
sweet. The sugar seemed to meld with the white

bread. Together they made a strange lump in my throat

        'It feels good to be back,' I said. 'I blew the welfare on beer & I was getting hungry'

        I kept staring at her black leather skirt. I took another bite of the sandwich

        I'd do it more slowly this time; I'd do it their way.

Maria

Never much needed a muse
when I had the beer; yet for so long
my fingers have been silent, the many days
of hospitalization have taken
something from me. I am
waiting
            I meet Maria
in the Nam restaurant; I have answered
her ad for companionship & sit uneasily
as she extracts my letter from a sheaf
of others. Her lips move
silently with each of my words; I study
the sharp lines of her face, find
the delicate silver earrings in her hair,
my eyes brush the cool skin
of her exposed shoulder. There are no words
for the way in which she lifts
the shrimp to her mouth. Maria is
an artists' model & she also paints
sometimes. I am lost
in the taste of black beans & pepper sauce,
my body cleansed of the weeks of hospital
fare
        After the meal, Maria
sips a European beer; I gulp
green tea, smoke cigarette after cigarette.
She talks of movies & painters; I probe
but do not penetrate, my words crumble
like ashes. Her eyes are somewhere else

We stand outside the restaurant
at a distance & say goodbye. I watch
her walk down College Street until
she is obscured by cars & passersby &
night. I know that I will never see her
again
      Late in the morning
I sit at my desk, stare out the window
at the street. This is the ludicrous
hour when poets & lovers have always come together,
alone. My books stand in alphabetical order
behind me. Uncertainly, my fingers
once again touch the keys of the typewriter.

JACK AND JILL
IN TORONTO

The Anti-Bourgeois

for Tracy in the Bahamas

A stupid paper cup
on a dirty glass shelf,
the name 'Millie'
scrawled on the outside
in black crayon:
inside, a few nickels and quarters.

I'm drunk
and getting drunker,
spending stolen money
and wasted Sunday afternoons
in the same taverns –
all of this because we drank
our weekend beer
on Saturday.

There's a little bit more.
I've got a bladder full of words:

don't stand in doorways.

Jack and Jill in Toronto

Jack and Jill were not killed
by their mishap;
though Jack now suffers migraines
for which he consults a psychologist on Tuesday
mornings while Jill attends her pottery class.
They
found out that it was the nitrates in the well
and now they have large bottles of spring water
delivered on Thursdays;
and they rarely fall.
But
Jack and Jill have a problem relationship
and are planning a trial separation:
they are going
to move into separate apartments but plan
to remain friends:
they both want to be writers
and need their own space.

Jill writes poetry,
though she doesn't like to call herself a poet,
and
she plans to write a series of poems about how
Jack controlled and brutalized her with his thing;
she
equates nature with freedom and their apartment
with oppression;
she is moving to the Annex and will buy
a number of large plants and no longer eat meat,
except

for fish occasionally.
                         Jack feels that he
is a very different kind of poet:
                                   he doesn't believe in
nature and will write his poems in the cafes,
                                        finding
in the streetlamps and passersby the images
for his emptiness and for the tragedy of his failed
love for Jill;
                    he will move into a different part
of the Annex;
                       he plans to take up reading when he
has the time.

            Both Jack and Jill have studied
the markets for poetry:
                         they know that,
                                        if only
they could get started,
                         they could do better.
                                        They
plan to write short imagistic pieces:
                                   Jack wants to
experiment with the way the words are placed upon
the paper;
            Jill will add psychological twists
to her poems.
                    If the small magazines won't take their
work,
       they plan to start their own
publications:
                    many of their friends have already

published small magazines.
But all of this will
take some time:
first their new apartments must be
set up,
their lives put back in order;
but already
Jack has signed up for a poetry-therapy workshop
and is planning his first piece;
and Jill has begun
to write in the journal she abandoned some years before.

Jack and Jill did eventually publish
several poems each,
and Jill in some of the more
respected magazines.
Jack later became an editor
for Maclean-Hunter publications and took up haiku
as a hobby;
Jill became too busy to write,
but
found her career as a social worker just
as satisfying.
They never saw each other again,
except
once at a distance,
at a poetry reading by 'Peggy'
Atwood.

This is a very sad story,
but it is non-violent
and it doesn't rhyme.

An Aging Ballet Dancer

Antoine places his fork down beside his uneaten
plate of quiche: 'I wish I had an appetite.'
His young lover sips from a glass of white wine
and gazes lazily across their restaurant.

The restaurant does a good business.
The public likes the avocado-green walls.
The public likes the prints from New York and Paris.
The public likes to know the old ballet dancer.

Two Poems on Espionage

1. Three Writers

A. locks his file cabinet because he
has nothing to hide. B. locks her
file cabinet because, if A.
is going to hide the fact that he
has nothing to hide, she cannot
leave herself vulnerable. C. locks
his file cabinet to hide this poem
which he has written about his friends
A. and B.

2. Lovers

C. and D. are lovers. They live
in a house with A. and B., who are also
lovers. All four keep diaries, scraps
of paper with notes, coded or incomp-
rehensible, poems, etc. hidden
from their respective lovers. (As
mentioned, A., B. and C. keep theirs
locked in file cabinets.) Nevertheless,
C. knows that A. and B. have read
these secret papers. He knows that
D. has read his. He knows this
because D. has written in her diary
that she has read C.'s diary. C.
knows this because he has read
D.'s diary. While all of this is known,
none of it can be spoken of.

                              On certain
afternoons, this is all that C. can know
of love affairs. Or of the strategies
of cold wars.

Things That I Have Put into My Asshole

Saliva and semen and butter and baby oil,
tongues and thumbs and fingers of women,
the cock of an old man,
the cock of a Mexican boy,
the cock of my sister's boyfriend,
my hand,
candles and felt marking pens,
cucumbers and carrots,
Sandra's mother's vibrator,
the intersection of Bathurst and Queen,
Honest Ed's Warehouse,
Hamilton Ontario,
and just today the CN Tower:

I came all over Bay Street,
as the world's highest disco
rotated upon my prostate.
YOU ARE NOW FREE, TORONTONIANS!
It lies limp on the frozen surface
of Lake Ontario.
You can barely see the tungsten bulbs
spelling 'Eat a lobster'
through the film of K-Y Jelly.
GO FREE, TORONTONIANS!
The small sacrifice
of a very large asshole.

This Summer in Rosedale

It was a nice day.

I took the Queen car to Yonge Street,
     ate a submarine sandwich, and, later,
     walked north.
Somehow I found myself in Rosedale.
I was drunk.

Crossing a street, I was almost struck
     by a black limousine which stopped
     with its nose two feet inside of the
     crosswalk.
'Death to drivers,' I screamed, pounding
     on the hood of the car.
The passenger of the car got out: it was
     Morley Callaghan.
'You almost killed me, you fat old bas-
     tard.'
He said nothing. I was mad.
'If you can punch that drunken suicide
     Hemingway, you can punch me,' I slurred.
'I'm an old man now,' Callaghan replied.
I stepped on his foot.
'I'm an old man and I've got a bad heart.'
I kneed him in the crotch.
'I'm an old man now,' he repeated.
I punched him in the face.

He fell back against the limousine.
My hand was broken.

Post-Modernism

I was standing on the empty platform
of a subway station in the suburbs
of Toronto, thinking about the status
of Modern Canadian Literature, of what
it meant to be A Canadian – my friends
had been asking why I hadn't shown them
any of my newer poems, and I didn't know
why – I wanted to make it big
in the Toronto Poetry Scene; but really
I was standing on the empty platform
getting drunk. There were all these ads
for different kinds of booze, big
colour photos of glasses with big cubes
of ice and lots of booze;
and I was getting very drunk just being there
and looking at them. And that was why
I fell down on the tracks – my friends know
my suicidal tendencies, but really
that is why I fell, I didn't jump –
but it doesn't matter
because I wasn't killed. My head, without
the brain, flew up from under the wheels
of the train and landed in a plastic bag
that was in the hand of an old wino
standing there – he didn't notice,
but in the morning he sold my head
as a window piece to a vegetarian café
on Queen Street, later drinking up the money
he had made in the Blue Jay Tavern
while telling this fantastic story.

The headless body, a bit bloody
I can tell you, went on to do a Ph.D.
in English Literature, and later gained
a teaching position in the Linguistics Dept.
of the University of Manitoba, and later still
wrote an important book on the correlation
between the prairie landscape and post-
modernist literature. You might ask
what happened to the brain. I told you about
the suicidal tendencies, and there are a lot
of things even I don't understand;
because long ago I took the brain and some
other parts I wasn't using much, wrapped
them in cellophane, and left them
in the meat department of a Loblaws store;
it seemed fair compensation for the three
cans of tuna I had stuffed in my pockets
and made off with. Dear Reader,
do you ever shop at Loblaws? I love you.

Love Poem

In the cool glimmer of a winter moon,
There lies the skeleton of my love.

One arm is chained to the bedpost.
The other holds the window open.

He simply quit eating one day.
Death was slow but satisfying for us both.

Yesterday, I rouged his rotting skull.
Now, a fly crawls from an eye socket.

I sit, smoking cigarettes,
And watch the semen run down the bone of his thigh.

Love Poem No. 2

O Syphilis, arise my love,
and we will go down to the streets
and beat a wild dance to the morning;
tear to shreds the stained sheets
where we have slept together
and come down to the morning bars
of Montreal and San Francisco,
and we will drink cold beer
from the bottle, in the morning bars
of New York and Mexico;
and I will rave like a zen lunatic,
for you are in my blood, my obsession;
I stink of you, I sweat of you

O Syphilis –
in tattered clothes and unwashed skin,
come down with me to the morning bars,
come down with me to the morning streets,
for who else will have me now

Hate Poem for Lauren

I hate you because I hate myself.

I hate you because I am drunk and cannot remember if I
loved you yesterday.

I hate you because you will not leave me to drink in peace.

I hate you because I hate my friends.

I hate you because I hate my family.

I hate you because I will forgive them all in moments
of terror.

I hate you because I hate my government.

I hate you because all of my acts and words are impotent
against it.

I hate you because I hate the rich who, for all of their money,
still live like shit.

I hate you because I hate the poor who spend their money on
beer instead of machine guns.

I hate you because I hate the working class, for their pettiness
and stupidity, and because they hate as well.

I hate you because we do not laugh aloud at the fascists and
treat them like children.

I hate you because anarchists sit bickering in fashionable
restaurants.

I hate you because I hate your family and the house that
they live in.

I hate you because a drunk lies on his back, feet kicking, in a
doorway.

I hate you because I do not help him up.

I hate you because I have stood in doorways, eyes drilling the
cement, my blood pounding like a hydraulic jack.

I hate you because the concrete did not burst.

I hate you because it did not rain.

I hate you because the exotic dancer, in the tavern where I
ate my lunch, had stick legs and tattoos on her thighs.
I hate you because I did not like the food I had to eat.
I hate you because I did nothing today.

I hate you because you love me.
I hate you because you wanted me and want me still.
I hate you because I will awake sick in the early morning and
compare your snoring face to the severed head of a fish
on ice.
I hate you because you are beautiful.
I hate you because my hand between your legs finds the
oozing of our unborn children.
I hate you because I do not want children.
I hate you because of the thousand nights we will lie together,
hating and loving.
I hate you because I did not desire you on the morning of
July 18, 1981.
I hate you because soon my liver will kill me.
I hate you because Jack Kerouac's stomach burst from the
same poison in his forty-seventh year as he watched the
Galloping Gourmet on television.
I hate you because I will die hating.
I hate you because everything that we tried and will try to
make perfect was and will be only what it was and will be.
I hate you because I love you.
I hate you because I can only know this in several moments
of drunkenness.
I hate you because I cannot believe in my disbelief.

Why Good Poems Are Never Written in Toronto

Some write their poems on streetcars,
or in libraries,
and some in university classrooms;
and some think of their poems
on downtown streets
and write them at desks later,
or before expensive beers at Harbourfront;
and others still write their poems
before windows in lonely apartments,
before lonely cups of coffee;
and then there are those
who leave the beds of lovers
and write their poems late into the night.

But none of those poems is ever good.

The good poems are written
early in the morning at a table
before a glass of brandy
or a glass of draught beer.
But the bars in Toronto do not open
before eleven in the morning
and some not before the noon hour:
our best poets are lined up in the streets
in the early morning,
and when they try to write their poems,
the rock band is often too loud.

Title Unknown

Your arm is still now.
An empty wine glass rests in your hand.

There is the meditation of the refrigerator.
Your clock radio broke one day.

The walls echo a battle of some other winter.
There are bloodstains on the bedsheets.

A cockroach skates across the floor.
It disappears beneath an unread newspaper.

You decide to go out for a drink.
You decide you are not thirsty.

Total blackness embraces the window.
The glass trembles slightly.

You are alone in this prison of stillness.
You've written these lines many times before.

Jack and Jill Go to an Anti-Cruise Demo

'They already have enough bombs to blow up
the world six times,' Jack exclaimed.
Jill only nodded her head, as her mouth was full
of cream cheese with sprouts on a dark bagel.
She took a sip of her No-Risk® fruit juice.
'I won't let them blow me up,' Jill said.

Jack was looking around at the thousands of people
on the lawn in front of the legislative buildings.
There were hundreds of different signs,
but Jack wasn't looking at those.
Jack was looking at all of the attractive women
that surrounded him.
Jack and Jill hadn't had sex recently – what
with the heat and all the pressure Jill had at work.
Jack was feeling very horny.
'This is just like a giant orgy,' Jack thought.
There were a lot of attractive women.
'I would like to have sex with all of these women,'
Jack thought.

Jill wasn't thinking much about bombs either.
She was thinking of her job
with the No-Risk® Fruit Juice Corporation.
Jill was a commercial designer with a background
in sociology.
She was supposed to figure out how to make people buy
certain things.
Right now she was supposed to think of a way to make
people buy the newest No-Risk® product, kiwi juice.

'How will I ever get them to buy kiwi juice,'
Jill was thinking.

Meanwhile, the crowd was getting excited.
'1-2-3-4,' they yelled, 'we don't want a nuclear war.'
'5-6-7-8,' the crowd roared, 'stop the bomb before
it's too late.'
'Before it's too late,' Jack and Jill echoed
as loudly as they could.
The crowd started to move towards the street.
Jack could hardly contain his mounting sexual excitement.
'This is like the most incredible orgy,' Jack thought.
Jill was so moved that there were tears in her eyes.
'Thousands of people all protesting together!'
she thought.
'Thousands of people all buying kiwi juice!'
she was thinking.
The crowd exploded onto the street.

That evening, Jack and Jill were very tired.
It had been a physically and emotionally exhausting day.
They decided to go to bed early.
'That was some march,' Jill said,
nestling up to Jack.
'We sure showed those bastards,' said Jack,
the blanket beginning to swell at his hips.
Jack and Jill had very good sex that night.
They tried a new position Jill had read about
in *Cosmopolitan* magazine.
Jack brought out an electric penis ring with
clitoral stimulator.
He had been hiding it in a drawer for weeks.

Several years passed
and Jack and Jill moved ahead rapidly at their jobs.
They had less and less time for peace activities.
They found it necessary to buy a car.
Jack was becoming heavily involved with video
and stereo electronics and needed more space.
They moved out of their apartment in the Annex
and found a renovated house in Cabbagetown.
Jack and Jill decided that they did not want
to bring children into this world,
it being the way it was,
with the threat of nuclear war and everything.
Their sex life was getting better all the time.
They had even discussed swinging,
which gave Jack something to think about
while masturbating in the washroom at his office.
Jack began to make videotapes of his lovemaking
with Jill,
and they would show them when friends dropped by.

And the moral of our story goes something like this:

Jack and Jill became more and more involved with
modern technology,
buying first a microwave oven and then a food processor.
Jack bought more expensive and up-to-date
video equipment and even a home computer.
Eventually they decided that cruise missiles
were the ultimate fuck.
And Jack and Jill lived happily ever after
within the capitalist system.

I Will Fall to My Knees and Bite Your Ankles, for I Must Be Holier Than Thou

The people I know are sick.
Each moment they worry at their eighty years of
    death as if it were a scab.
They have a hundred diseases and a hundred specialists and
    therapists to propagate each.
Our conversations are endless: the progress of
    bowels and penises and vaginas and stomachs
    and lungs and brains and psyches and souls
    and nerves and eyes and sexualities and on
    and on ...
We live in a hospital for the impoverished:
    instead of in beds, we lie waiting in our
    coffins.
And the internment is killing us: we have shrivelled
with pettiness; even our hatreds are
    small ones.
We cannot see out of the window: we spend our
    days in individual and collective psycho-
    logical attacks.
Kicks and punches are not allowed by our rules
    of etiquette.
Death must be slow: we want to live.

Mornings like these, I would embrace Reagan
and Andropov like brothers, if for one
moment my hatred could blossom, as beautiful
as a mushroom cloud.

The people I know are sick, and I write sick poems.

TWO COPS

KISSING

Preface

The summer of 1982 found me washing dishes, not writing but drinking heavily & living in a basement bachelor in downtown Toronto. Often, in the evenings, I would sit on the steps of the apartment building, drinking cheap wine & rediscovering the works of Jack Kerouac. In the ramblings of Kerouac & Gary Snyder (as recorded in *The Dharma Bums*) I found a direction out of my current sense of emptiness – zen buddhism & the composition of haiku. While my experiments with zen philosophy & meditation proved futile, my interest in haiku was enriched by a wide reading of traditional & contemporary Japanese haiku in translation. That same summer I enrolled in a haiku workshop given by George Swede at Ryerson. For the next few months I dedicated myself to the writing of haiku, documenting within the structures of the English haiku tradition certain high & low moments of my tired existence in a large & varied metropolis.

That autumn I somehow found myself in the role of secretary of the Haiku Society of Canada. I spent the next several months organizing a massive reading of haiku which would take place at Harbourfront & which would feature the best-known writers of haiku from across Canada. During this period I met with & read the work of many prominent North American haikuists. Rather than encouraging me, this brought about my complete disillusionment with haiku. What I discovered was a mass of hobbyists imitating translations of centuries-old Japanese haiku. Everywhere the subject matter was foreign to that of contemporary North American existence. Clearly most of the poets I read had not even discovered the modernism of contemporary Japanese haiku. The few haikuists who were doing anything original were completely bogged down in lifeless explorations of form & linguistics.

When it was my turn to take the stage at Harbourfront the following spring, I drunkenly & somewhat pathetically lashed out at the audience: *Do you really want to hear this crap?* Some people I know remember my performance fondly; I'm sure that many of the haikuists present remember it otherwise. I've never written a haiku since nor read one nor had any intercourse with other Canadian haikuists. The haiku selected for this book are the best of those which I wrote in that period of approximately one year. Take 'em or leave 'em.

Jones
College Street, Toronto, 1984

Two Cops Kissing

After love,
the click of june bugs
against the glass

.

Dead geraniums
in a cracked clay pot:
I light my pipe

.

Also in the ditch,
a rooster screams:
my bowels make thunder

   Mexico 1980/82

.

Two cops kissing
in a tavern doorway:
delirium tremens

.

The sun breaks from cloud:
rain has made
her makeup run

.

Pigeons squat
on the crumbling statue:
cars pass

.

Chestnuts smacking
the roof of the car –
we start for Mexico

.

June bugs
strike at the lighted window ...
others follow

.

Striking the streetlamp
again and again, a moth
joins our parting

.

Her chin hairs stuck
to her chin –
we drink flat beer

.

Eating candy floss ...
until we come to the crushed
cat in the road

.

A dog in the spil-
led garbage eat-
ing my hangover

.

My lover fights
her constipation:
Toronto summer

.

An old shoe
against the wall of an alley,
worn again by leaves

.

Winter morning:
empty wire cart down Bathurst Street,
an old woman steering

.

All day the droning
of lawn mowers ...
and now only crickets

•

     Spring morning:
into the empty tavern
       struts a pigeon

•

Summer afternoon:
a broken neon sign argues
with cicadas

•

Plum blossoms!
He removes them from the tread
of his Adidas

•

Cold evening wind:
I give a wino
my last cigarette

•

Choked with leaves,
a pumpkin staring up
from beside the road

.

Out of car windows,
loud music ...
I vomit Bathurst Street

.

After the rally,
pigeons gather
among discarded leaflets

.

The blind man drops
his cane in the street
    – a sound like a gunshot

.

Foggy morning:
    the street-sweeper rubbing
    and rubbing his eyes

.

Clothing-factory women
reading paper bibles:
streetcar at dawn

·

Sunday afternoon:
beside a bloated hammock,
lawn sprinklers whisper

·

How perfect the sadness
of these wilting lilacs:
thoughts of Jane's lips

·

How silent the night.
In this deserted kitchen,
a turkey carcass

Afterword

The manuscript that would become *The Brave Never Write Poetry* was hauled off the slush pile at Coach House Press by David W. McFadden, and by the time it was published in the fall of 1985, its depressive alcoholic author, at twenty-six, had stopped drinking for good. I was a few years younger than Jones when I reviewed it in my fledgling literary magazine, *What!* That turned out to be pretty much the only positive review the book would receive – a shame given how gifted Jones clearly was, and how unusual his accounts of depression, drinking and doomed love still seem today in the context of Canadian poetry.

For some reason Canada has never been kind to its confessional poets. I'm not sure you can explain the aversion without tripping over some indefensible generalization about emotional reticence and the national character. But the fact is virtually every reviewer who encountered *The Brave* disliked it. They complained about Jones's tired drunken-poet 'persona.' They dismissed the direct, unadorned language as just cut-up prose. They winced at all the references to sex and booze and bodily fluids. They bitched about the supposed self-indulgence of Jones's introduction, his pretentious use of his last name only, even the fact the book included multiple photographs of the author. I haven't been able to find the review, but Gil Adamson, who was a summer intern at Coach House and did the publicity on *The Brave*, distinctly recalls one reviewer using the phrase 'I hate this author.'

Looking back at my own review – which marked the beginning of what would be an eight-year friendship with Jones – I'm surprised at how grudging even I was with my praise. Part of it was likely jealousy. Every young poet in Toronto wanted a Coach House book (I wouldn't get mine until 1995) and here was this *enfant terrible* from Hamilton writing about puke and semen and drunk tanks beating us all to the punch.

But the talent was obvious, and to dump on this debut collection for its few flaws would have been redundant by that point. I still think there are a few bad poems here, and the odd bad line in some of the others. But there's also an unadorned grace to these snapshots of wasted youth and a stunning emotional honesty that can't be faked:

> There is no terror
> There is
> nothing
>
> Give it back to us now, give
> it whatever it is, as beautiful, as
> brutal, as meaningless
> Give it back
> whoever you are
> billboard signs, shopping
> malls, fire engines & the night.
>
> ('Benzedrine')

I recognized the self-consciousness of Jones's battered persona, but I was so distracted by the grot and gore I failed to fully appreciate the gallows humour. More than anything now, these poems strike me as terribly funny. Jones's lampooning of the wannabe poets in the 'Jack and Jill' poems, and of cultural institutions in 'Work' are chillingly close to the truth as I remember it, just as the falseness of the backyard dinner party in 'Steaks' would feel like satire if I hadn't endured similar evenings. And then there are the scenes in detox centres and emergency wards, as in 'Sweating It Out':

> ... every few minutes
> a nurse takes my pulse
>   'How'd ya
> get yourself like this so young?'
> she wants to know
>   'It wasn't
> easy'

In 'White Bread,' the fact the patient finds his doctor sexy is darkly funny, first because it's an idiotic cliché the poet is well aware of, and second because his hands are shaking so hard he can barely hold a sandwich.

> 'I can't eat this shit,' I
> said
>   'That's pretty funny coming from someone who
> just tried to kill himself' ...

That Jones doesn't always give himself the punchline shows wisdom beyond his years, and his use of humour affords him some leeway during the poem's more emotional moments. The last lines: 'I'd do it more slowly this time; I'd do it their way,' are more chilling now in light of the poet's early death, but it's a great ending nonetheless.

Younger readers than me might be forgiven for thinking some of the irony and negativity in these poems a little excessive. In fact, this book reflects rather faithfully the hopelessness that prevailed in those days. Jobs were scarce, artists (especially poets) lived like cockroaches, punk music was still the rage among 'serious' people, and with Ronald Reagan the newly minted U.S. president, the Cold War seemed as dangerous a staring match as ever. Melodramatic? Perhaps. But terms like 'mutually assured destruction' were part of the argot. Small wonder most of us thought it was even money we'd perish in some fiery nuclear maelstrom.

Jones's nihilism ran deeper still, exacerbated as it was by depression and addiction (well-documented in his introduction). But I never met the Tear-off Jones, the person he writes about here and in the remarkable ultra-minimalist stories he published later. He was the most unlikely of intellectuals – a blue-collar kid from a blue-collar town who spent much of his adolescence and early adulthood either shitfaced or trembling in detox centres and emergency wards. And yet he'd been a bit of an art star at his Hamilton high school, having had two of his plays successfully produced before he graduated. He ultimately abandoned the degree he started at the University of Toronto, but he won the Norma Epstein Award for poetry as an undergraduate, twice.

By the late eighties he smoked French cigarettes, wore a scarf and a beret, and was always toting around a translation of some slim volume by Robbe-Grillet or Calvino. He'd assembled an impressive collection of first editions which he kept shelved alphabetically in protective acetate covers in the living room of his epic apartment on College Street. It was one of those turn-of-the-century caverns over a store designed to house an extended family. The kitchen was huge; there were two bathrooms; the living room alone was the size of most bachelor apartments. There was one bedroom used only as a kind of closet, another served as storage for bicycles.

Jones preferred Beckett and Genet, but unlike most of the people with strong opinions on the new theory, he had actually read Foucault and Derrida and Bloom and bell hooks. He considered himself a Marxist. He was a great proofreader and his office was the neatest of any writer I've ever met. All of his drafts were numbered and filed. His pencils were lined up on one side of a block of paper which was lined up next to the typewriter. Given what he wrote about, such fastidiousness was nothing short of bizarre.

Publicly, Jones laughed off criticism of *The Brave* as backhanded compliment. None of these clowns knew what they were talking about and wasn't it common knowledge Canadian poetry was run by philistine careerists and mediocrities? But deep down, it must have hurt. When a book of poetry sells, no one, including the publisher, is exactly sure why. It may have been because Jones did so many readings (and was such a good reader), or because the chorus of disapproval prompted the curious to pick up the book and decide for themselves. For whatever reason, the book sold out and has been notoriously hard to find in the twenty-plus years it has been out of print.

That fact alone provided one compelling rationale for a new edition. Another was an awareness that Jones could not have picked a worse time to publish this particular book if he'd tried. In 1985 poetry was painfully out of fashion – most of us wouldn't even admit we were poets in mixed company. I used to joke that in terms of public prestige, poets resided about one notch above mimes.

Canadian poetry at that time was factional to say the least. The academy was in love with post-structuralist theory and American 'Language Poetry.' Lyricism, weaned on twenty years of cultural nationalism and identity politics, had become predictable, complacent, in dire need of a renovation. The spoken-word movement had turned poetry performances into farcical affairs where writers with A-A-A rhyme schemes competed for beer money in so-called 'poetry sweatshops.' And into all that dropped this unguarded, vaguely romanticized collection of post-punk studies in suicide and depression, alienation and addiction. No one knew what to make of it.

Soon after *The Brave* was published, Jones found his given name and switched to fiction. For years he disowned the book completely. He never published another poem. If he even wrote one, he never showed it to me. Towards the end of his life, though, I sensed a softening on this front. I had reread *The Brave* multiple times in my early thirties, liking it better each time. I told Jones as much, and though he insisted I was crazy, I think he was secretly pleased.

A part of me wonders if Jones would be pissed at us for bringing this book back into print. I'd like to think I could have talked him into it, but not without extensive revision, and there's where it would have been tricky. There are at least three things that make for memorable poetry: invention (or, more simply, surprise), virtuosity and emotional risk. *The Brave* has some of each, but it has that last element in spades. In his fiction, Jones removed absolutely anything that smacked of sentiment – his prose is so spare it seems downright brittle at times. That same approach would have ruined these poems.

Like most good writers, Jones was amenable to editing – so much so you had to remind him he needn't agree with every suggestion. Reading these poems again, I was tempted to deep-six one or two of the aforementioned 'bad' poems, and to make small changes elsewhere I could be more or less sure Jones would have gone along with. But in the end I felt the book is what it is, flaws and all, mindful of the review I'd written when I was twenty-three: 'Some of the pieces ... fall into cliché and melodrama. Taken separately, they don't work, yet in the context of the whole collection they are somehow indispensible.'

The current state of Canadian poetry is much different from the one Jones had to navigate in 1985. There's a lot more going on, the battle lines between genres and factions have blurred or have even disappeared altogether. There's also a burgeoning interest in what was happening in the 1980s: in art, in writing and especially in music. As much as *The Brave Never Write Poetry* is a product of its time, the issues it addresses – depression, underemployment, addiction, alienation from the political process – remain relevant for people who are the same age now as Jones was when he wrote the poems.

I can't know if this new edition will earn the readership and respect a lot of us felt it deserved the first time. That's the hope, anyway. What I will say is that if a manuscript this good arrived at Coach House in the mail this week, written by a twenty-six-year-old, I'd be all over it.

Kevin Connolly
Toronto, March 2011

Jones

(Daniel) Jones was born in a working-class district of Hamilton in 1959. He moved to Toronto in 1977 to study at the University of Toronto, where he won two Norma Epstein Awards for poetry before abandoning his degree and becoming a writer and editor. His sole full collection of poems, *The Brave Never Write Poetry* (Coach House, 1985), appeared when its author was just twenty-six. Jones contributed to several Canadian magazines, acting as contributing editor for *Piranha* and *What!*, and later, editor-in-chief of *Paragraph*. He was also the author of two novels, *Obsessions: A Novel in Parts* (Mercury, 1992) and the posthumously published *1978* (Rush Hour Revisions, 1998), about the death of Toronto's punk scene. His collection of linked short stories, *The People One Knows,* was published in 1994, shortly after the author took his own life.

Typeset in Lyon Text and Futura

Edited by Kevin Connolly
Designed by Kevin Connolly and Alana Wilcox, after Depero
Author photo on page 1 by Sam Kanga

'

Coach House Books
80 bpNichol Lane
Toronto ON M5S 3J4

416 979 2217
800 367 6360

mail@chbooks.com
www.chbooks.com